The Armor of God Crafts and More

by Mary Currier

Illustrated by Corbin Hillam

Cover Illustrated by Corbin Hillam

A Division of Frank Schaffer Publications, Inc.
23740 Hawthorne Blvd., Torrance, CA 90505

ISBN No. 0-7647-0496-6

Table of Contents

ARMOR OF GOD

To Teachers and Parents

Soldiers need not only a uniform; they must also be well trained for battle. A soldier in any army must know what to do in times of peace and must be so well trained that he or she will act instinctively in times of battle. A good soldier's goal in life is being loyal and serving his or her commander. A soldier's lifestyle may be different because he or she has different motivations.

It is important that we, as Christians, give our children the "uniform" of a Christian. We must train them to be loyal to the One we serve and alert to the devil's deceitful and tricky ways. We must show them how to stay away from this world's evil temptations and stay true to God who made us and is our only hope of salvation. We must teach our children that a Christian soldier must follow all the Commander's orders, not just pick and choose which ones he or she wants to follow. We need to help our children put their trust and love in Jesus.

The activities in this book have been designed to help children have fun learning how to be good soldiers of Christ. They include crafts, songs, games, bulletin boards, posters, and much more. As you use each activity, be sure to emphasize the truths it teaches. Most of the crafts can be taken home after they are completed. Encourage the children to share their crafts with their families and explain to them what the craft teaches or reminds us to do.

While many of the activities in this book are based directly on Ephesians 6, the Armor of God passage in the Bible, some are based on other Scripture passages or verses. However, each activity indirectly relates to the life of the Christian soldier and the armor God has available for him or her.

"Stand Against Evil" Wheel

This wheel is the perfect craft for you to make to help you stand strong against evil.

1. Color and cut out the wheels on this page and page 5.
2. Insert a brass fastener to fasten the smaller wheel on top of the larger one.
3. Turn the top wheel until a problem (such as "idolatry") appears in the cut-out arrow. Ask the Lord to help you with this sin if it is a problem in your life. You can fight against sin in your life through faith in Jesus.

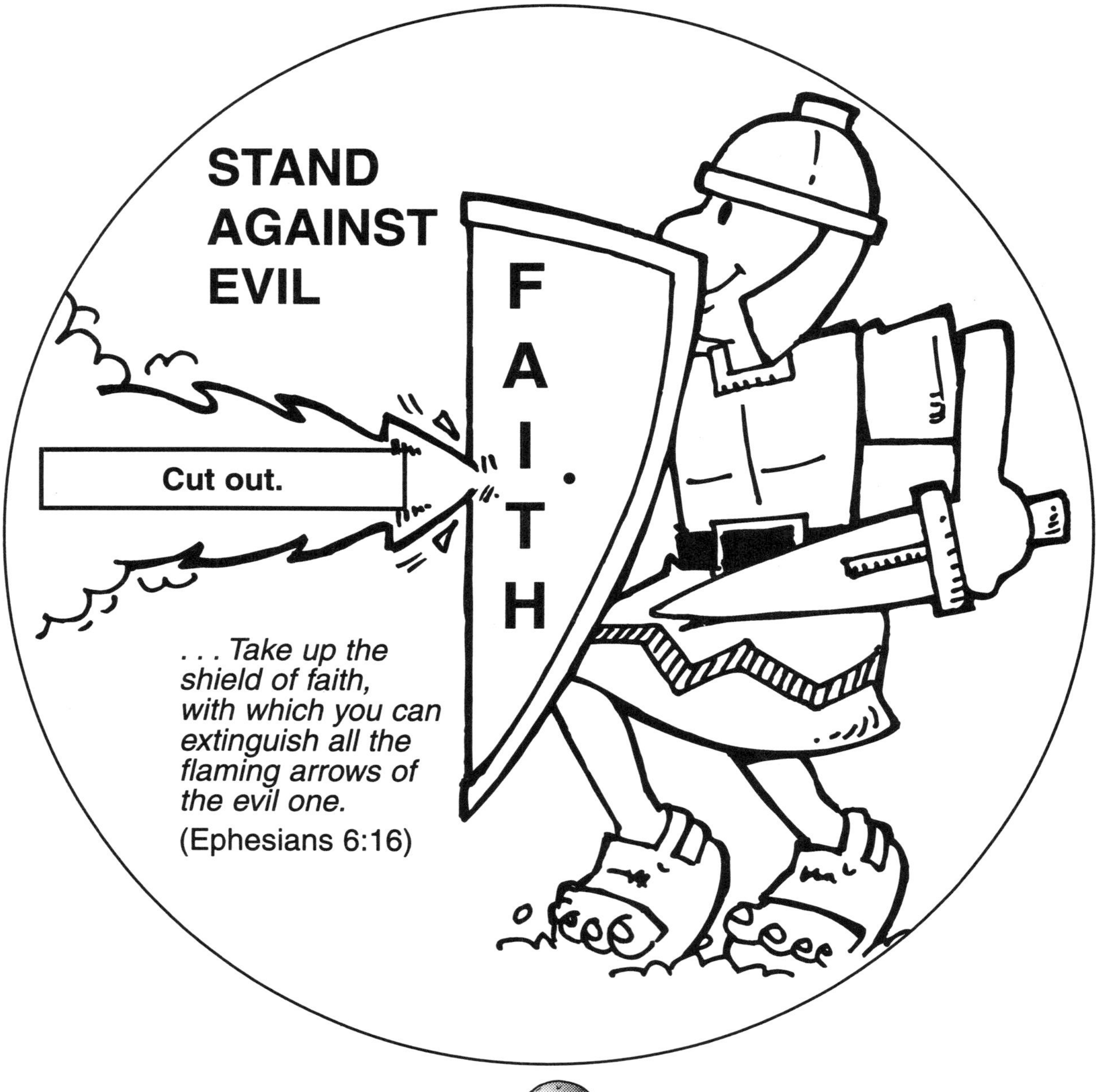

STAND AGAINST EVIL

FAITH

Cut out.

. . . Take up the shield of faith, with which you can extinguish all the flaming arrows of the evil one.
(Ephesians 6:16)

"Stand Against Evil" Wheel

Ask God to Help You

Ask God to Help You

Ask God to Help You

Ask God to Help You

Ask God to Help You

Ask God to Help You

"Do not be afraid . . . I am your shield . . ." Genesis 15:1

But you are a shield around me, O Lord . . . Psalm 3:3

The Lord is my strength and my shield . . . Psalm 28:7

SMOKING

DRUGS

ALCOHOL

LOVE OF PLEASURE

DISHONESTY

LOVE OF MONEY

HATE

IMPURITY

IDOLATRY

DISOBEDIENCE

SELFISHNESS

TEMPTATION

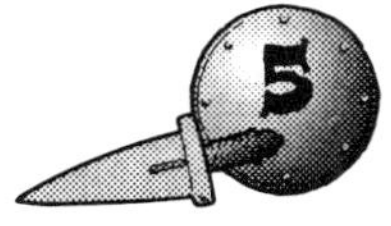

"Put on the Whole Armor" Song

(tune: "On Top of Old Smoky")

Sing this song every morning to remind yourself to wear God's armor each day.

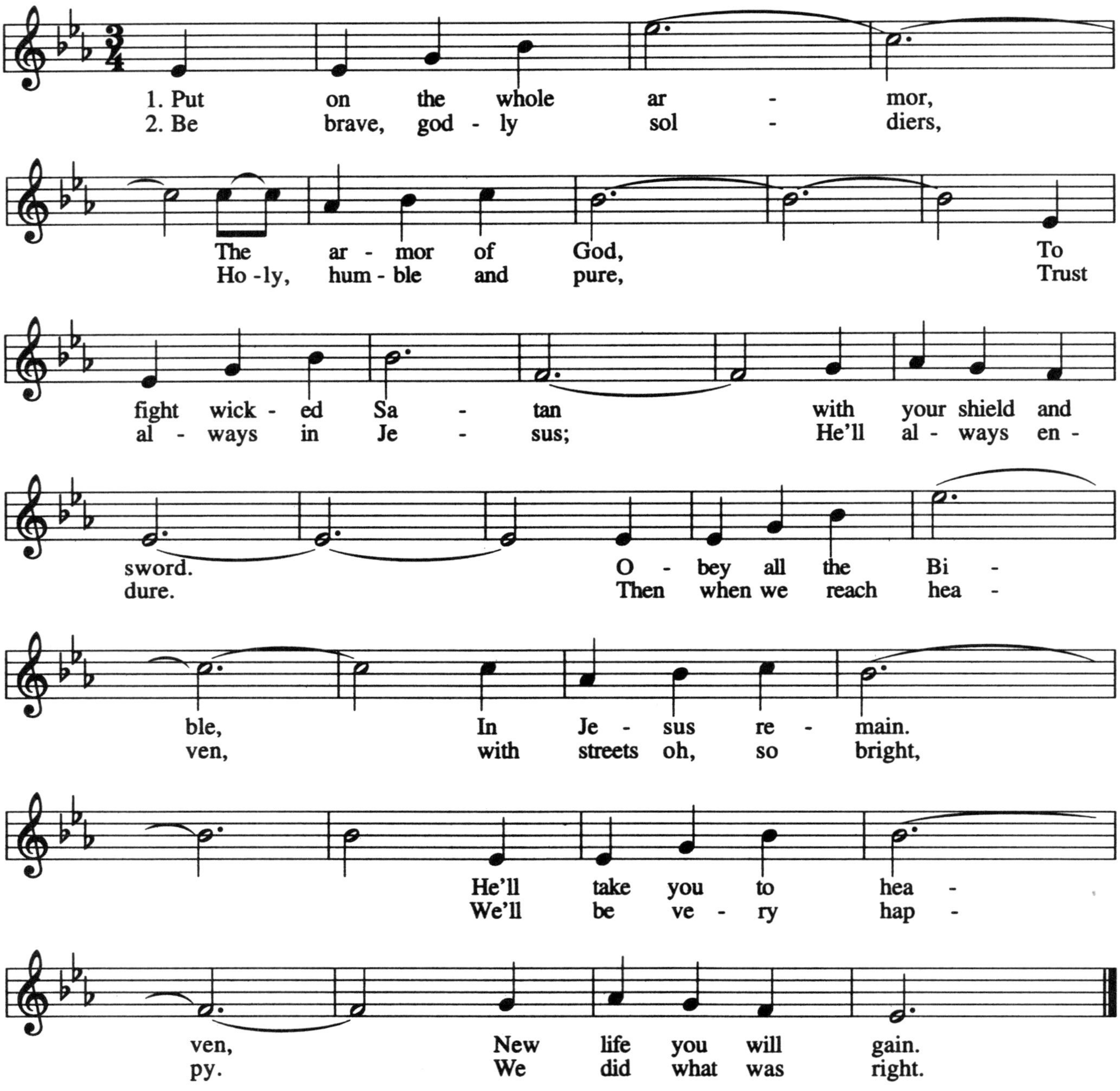

1. Put on the whole ar - mor,
2. Be brave, god - ly sol - diers,

The ar - mor of God, To
Ho -ly, hum - ble and pure, Trust

fight wick - ed Sa - tan with your shield and
al - ways in Je - sus; He'll al - ways en -

sword. O - bey all the Bi -
dure. Then when we reach hea -

ble, In Je - sus re - main.
ven, with streets oh, so bright,

He'll take you to hea -
We'll be ve - ry hap -

ven, New life you will gain.
py. We did what was right.

Soldier Clothespin Craft

We need to follow Jesus no matter how rough the road. Jesus said, *"Whoever serves me must follow me . . ."* (John 12:26a) Are you following Jesus, trying to do what He wants you to do? Make this craft as a reminder to follow Jesus. Keep it in your room where you can see it every day.

1. Color the figure and cut it out.
2. Clamp two clothespins on the soldier's horse for legs.

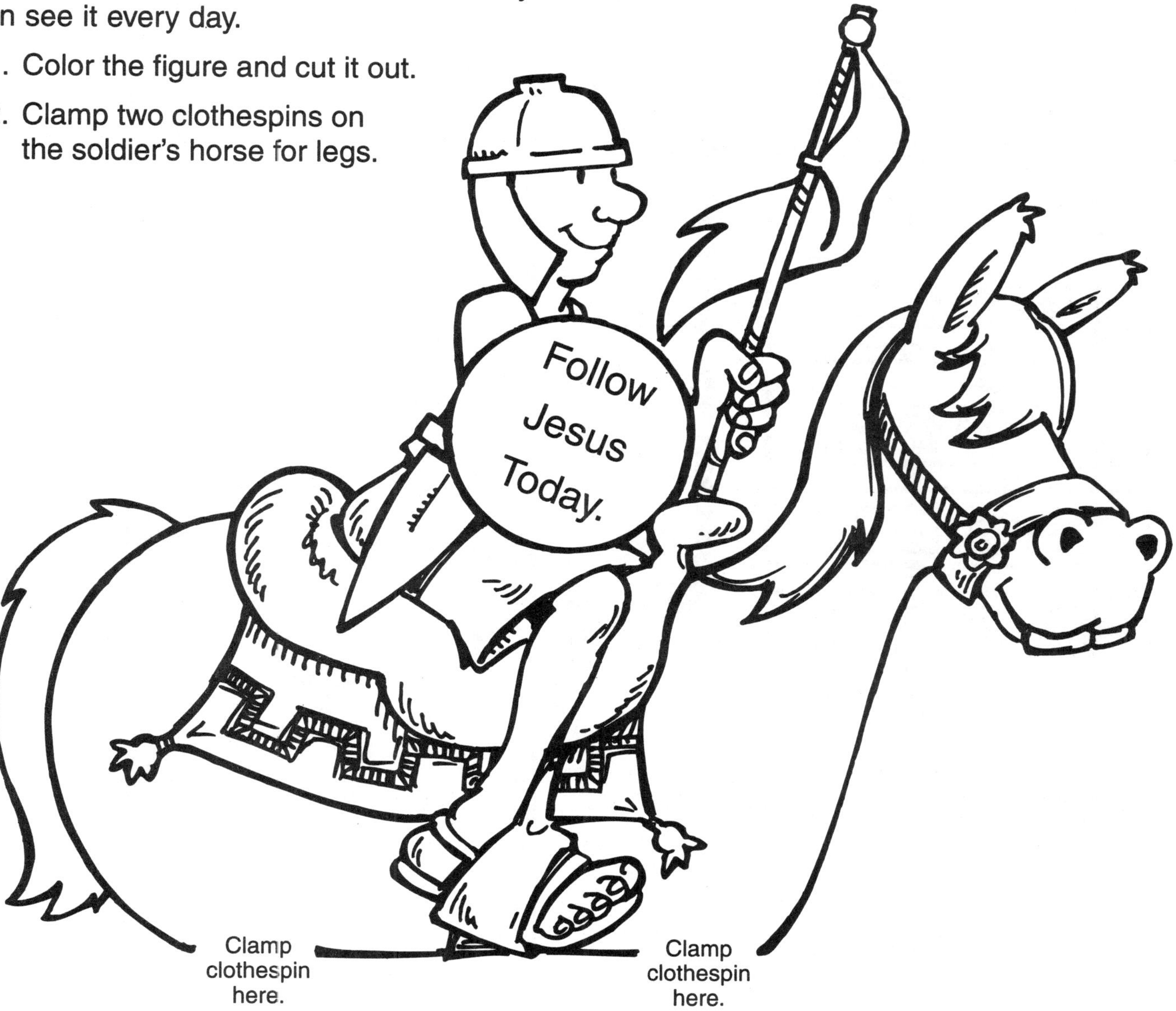

Follow Jesus Today.

Clamp clothespin here.

Clamp clothespin here.

Bible Memory Badge

1. Color and cut out the badge and the memory strips below.
2. Use a pin to fasten the badge to your shirt.
3. Every time you memorize one of the verses, glue another strip on your badge.

tab A

Ephesians 6:10

Ephesians 6:11

Ephesians 6:12

Ephesians 6:13

Ephesians 6:14

Ephesians 6:15

Ephesians 6:16

Ephesians 6:17

Ephesians 6:18

Your Name

I AM A
SOLDIER
IN THE
ARMY
OF THE
KING
OF
KINGS!

Glue tab A here.

Peace Shoes

Wear these shoes of peace proudly and spread God's love!

1. Glue the shoes on heavy paper.
2. Color and cut out the shoes. (Be sure to cut out the center and the small holes for the shoestrings.)
3. Slip each shoe over your foot. Thread a 12" piece of yarn or string into each hole and tie.

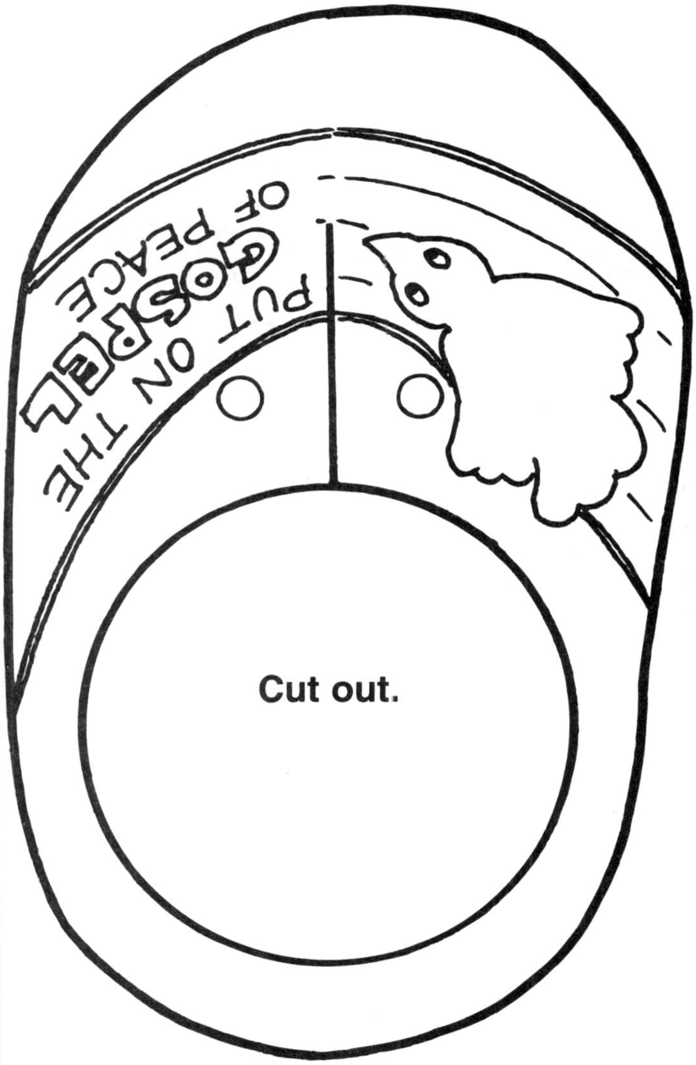

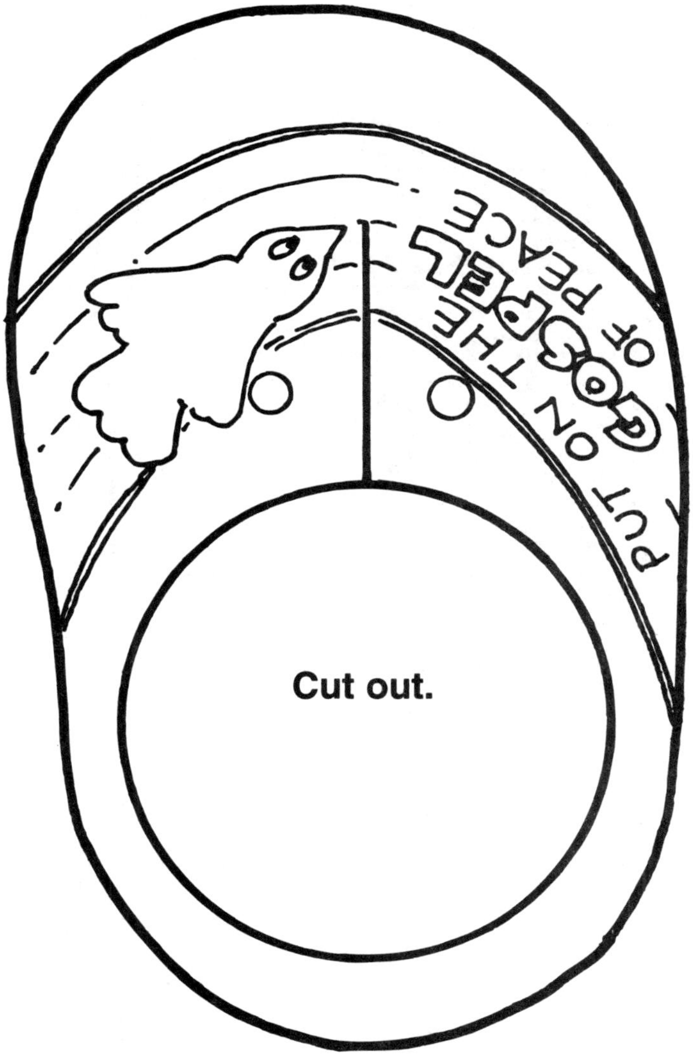

PUT ON THE GOSPEL OF PEACE

Cut out.

PUT ON THE GOSPEL OF PEACE

Cut out.

Paper Doll Soldier

Make the paper doll soldier using the patterns below and on page 11. Dress him in his armor to help you remember the armor God wants you to use to fight the devil.

1. Glue the soldier and his armor on heavy paper.
2. Color the soldier and the armor pieces and cut them out.
3. Fold the tabs on the pieces of armor.
4. Put the armor on the soldier.

RIGHTEOUSNESS

FAITH

TRUTH

Paper Doll Soldier Patterns

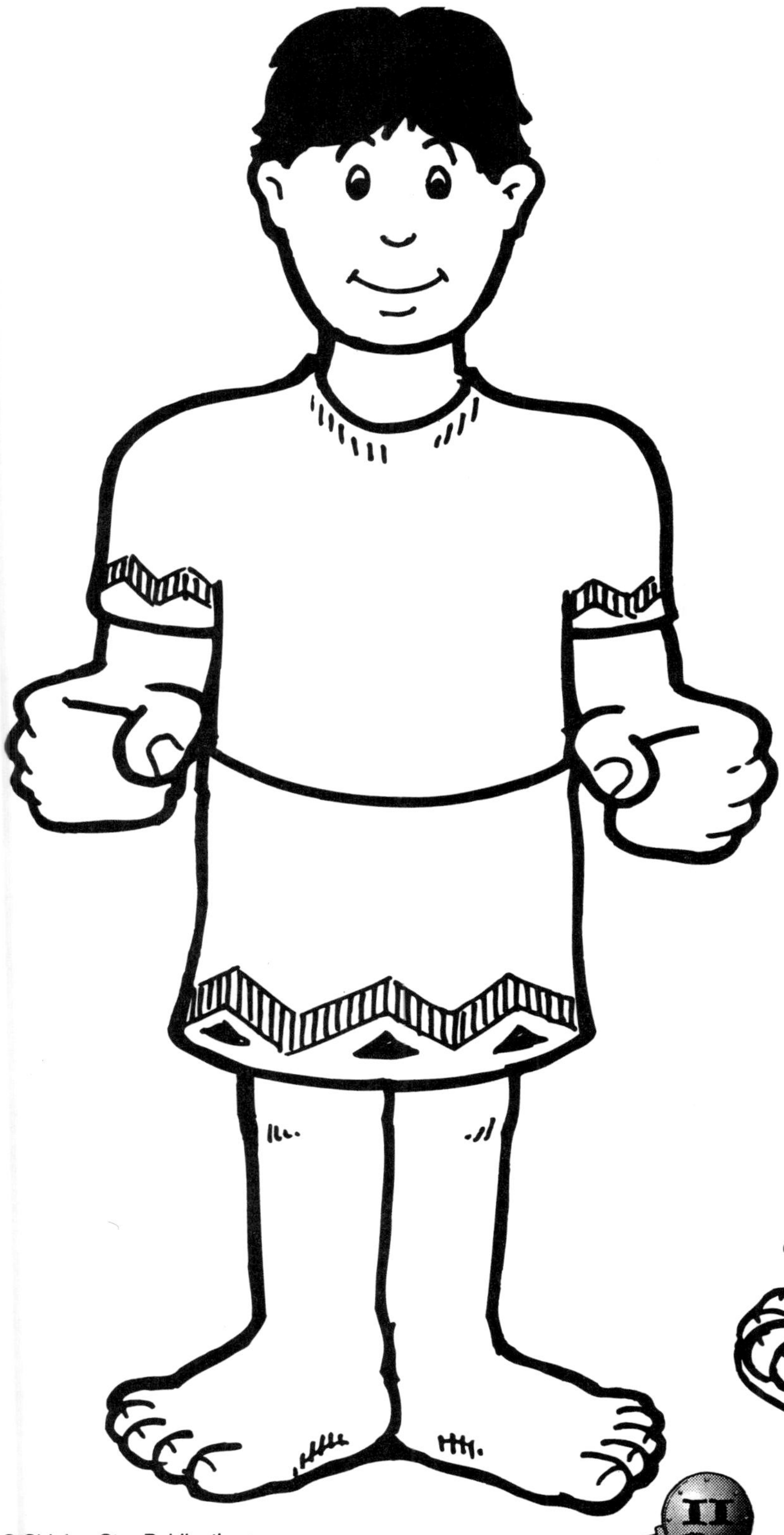

SALVATION

WORD OF GOD

PEACE

Soldier Face Mask

Make the mask below and put it on when you need to be reminded to stand strong against evil.

1. Color and cut out the mask. (Be sure to cut out the eyeholes.)
2. Tie two 12" lengths of string in holes you have punched on the sides of the mask. Adjust the strings to fit your head and tie them.

Jesus
is
our
only
SALVATION!

Cut out.

Cut out.

Buckle Up for Truth

Wear this belt of truth to show that you want to live by God's Word!

1. Color the belt.
2. Cut it out around the edge and on the heavy lines. (Be careful to stay on the lines. Don't cut too far.)
3. Open up the belt and slip it over your head and down to your waist.

Buckle Up with

TRUTH

Christian Soldier's Code Book

Now you can be a good Christian soldier, too. Just follow the directions below.

1. Cut out the code book on the solid lines.
2. Fold on the dotted lines.
3. Use the code to discover the directions for being a good Christian soldier.

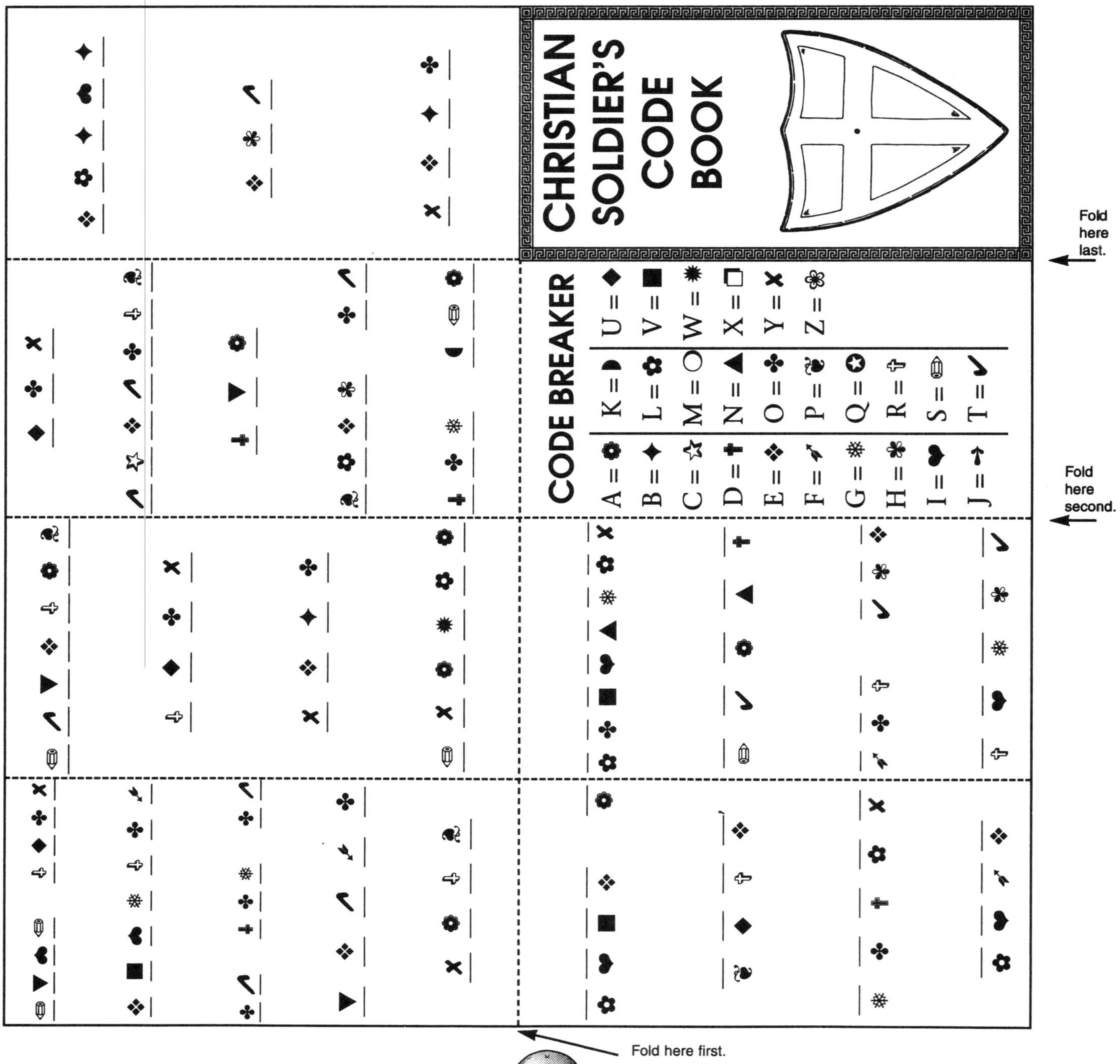

CHRISTIAN SOLDIER'S CODE BOOK

Fold here last.

CODE BREAKER

A =
B =
C =
D =
E =
F =
G =
H =
I =
J =
K =
L =
M =
N =
O =
P =
Q =
R =
S =
T =
U =
V =
W =
X =
Y =
Z =

Fold here second.

Fold here first.

Bookmarks

These bookmarks will remind you to be true to God.

1. Color and cut out the bookmarks.
2. Cover them with clear plastic adhesive, front and back.
3. Punch holes where shown.
4. Thread a 6" length of yarn through each hole and tie a knot.

I will stay true to my Lord and King. The Lord will protect all around me.

Without faith, it is impossible to please Him.

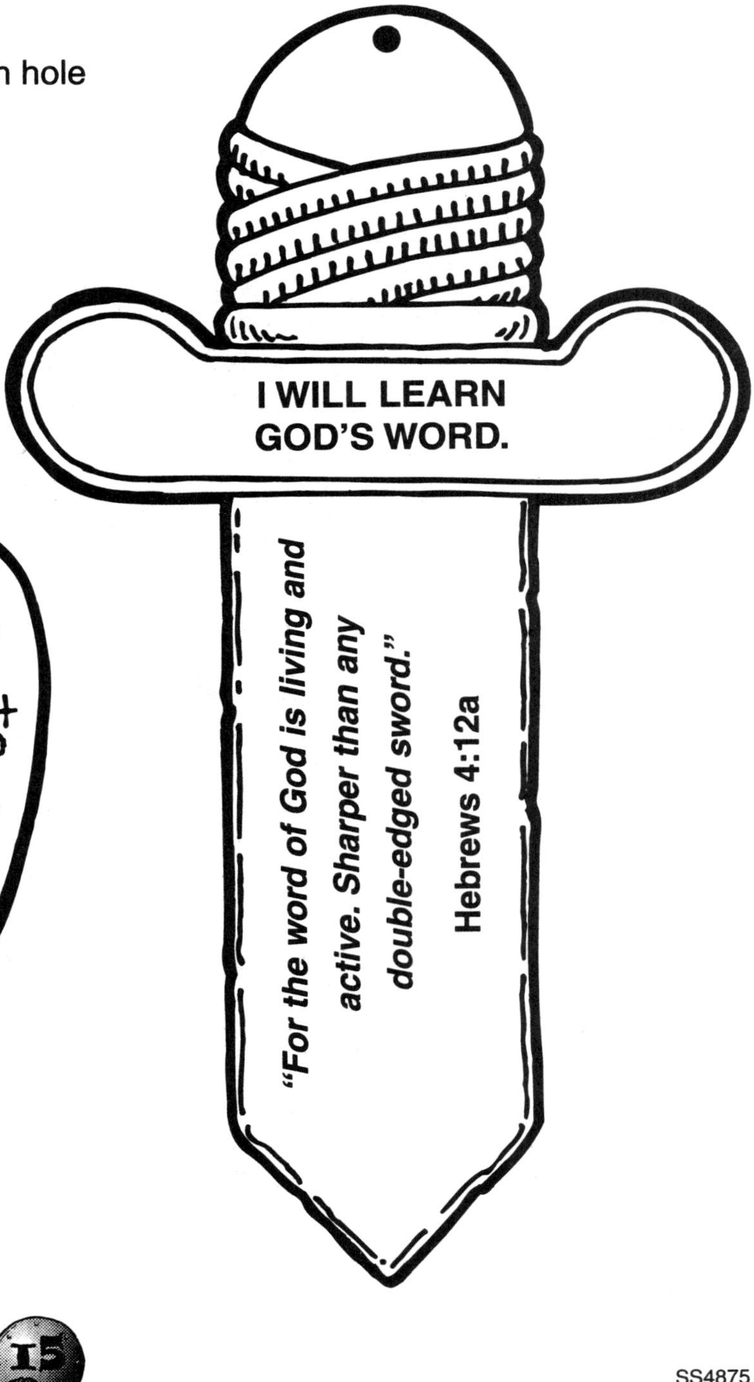

I WILL LEARN GOD'S WORD.

"For the word of God is living and active. Sharper than any double-edged sword."

Hebrews 4:12a

Wanted Poster

Hang this poster in your room to remind you that God always wants you to follow His Word!

1. With a brown crayon, color lightly around the edge of the poster on page 17.
2. Tear along the edge to make it ragged and old-looking.
3. Curl the corners forward by wrapping them around a pencil.
4. Glue the poster onto a sheet of brown construction paper, leaving the corners curled.

GOD WANTS YOU

Volunteer Now: Choose God's side.*"Now is the day of salvation."* (2 Corinthians 6:2b) *"Unless you repent, you too will all perish."* (Luke 13:3)

Only sincere applicants please.

Full Armor Provided: (Ephesians 6:11–17) Armor is given for battles fought throughout life. A pure white robe will be given after the battles of life are over.

Must Enlist for Life: No deserters. To win the reward, you must endure to the end.

Victory Guaranteed: God gives us the victory through Jesus Christ our Lord.

REWARDS

* Eternal Life (Romans 6:23)
* Peace that passes all understanding (Philippians 4:7)
* Crown of Life (Revelation 2:10)

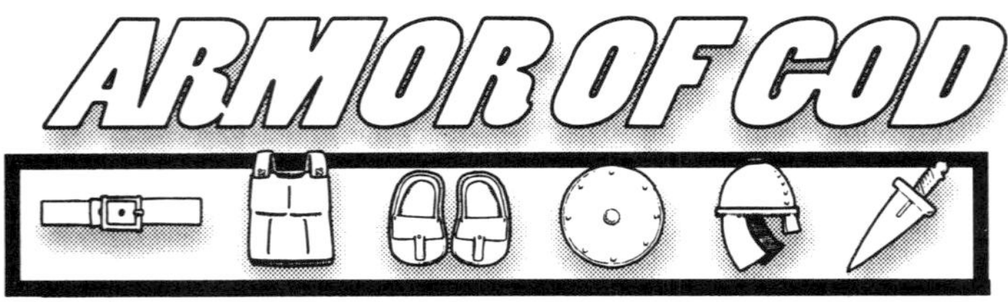

Sword Memory Verse Tool

This sword can be a powerful weapon to help you memorize God's Word.

1. Color the sword.
2. Cut out the sword on the heavy lines.
3. Glue the sword to posterboard and cut it out.
4. Cover the sword with clear plastic adhesive, front and back.
5. Cut out the Bible verses on page 19.
6. Staple a verse to the sword where shown.
7. Use the sword to memorize God's Word.

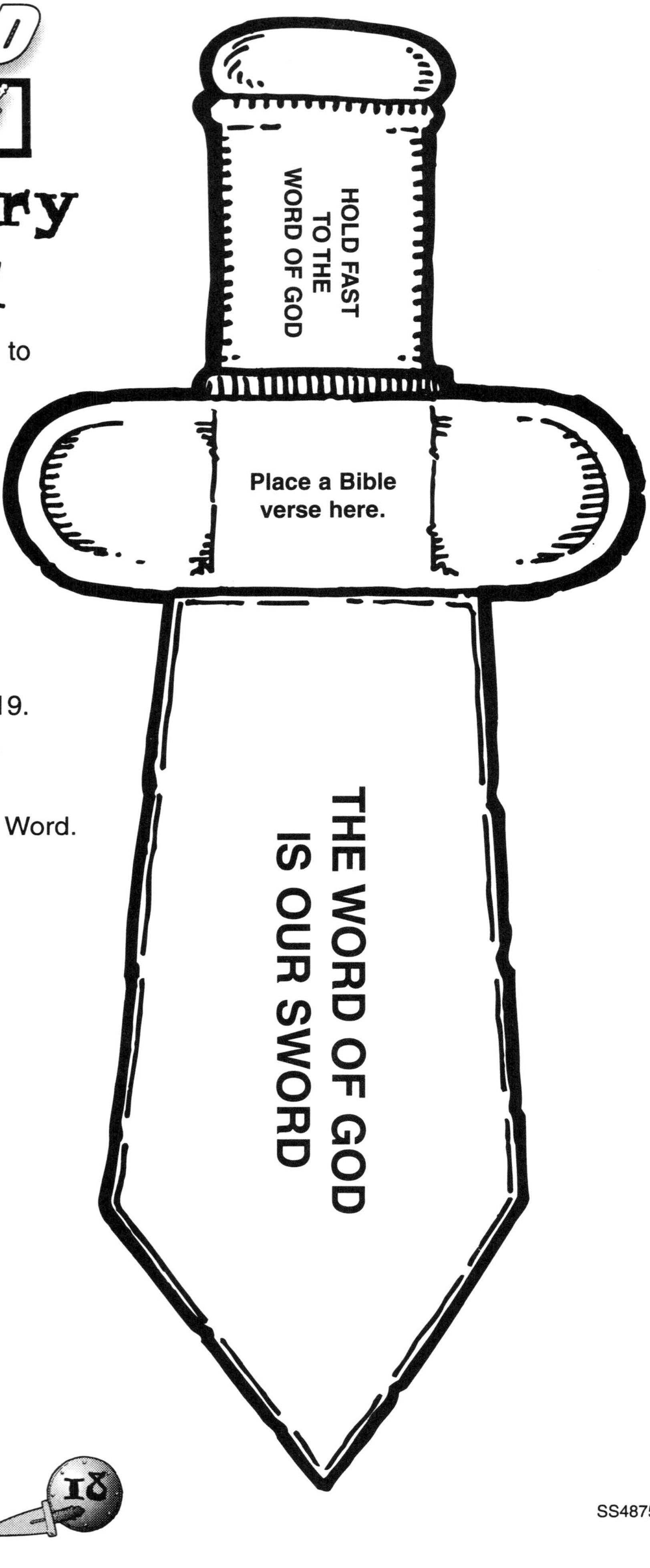

HOLD FAST TO THE WORD OF GOD

Place a Bible verse here.

THE WORD OF GOD IS OUR SWORD

Memory Verses

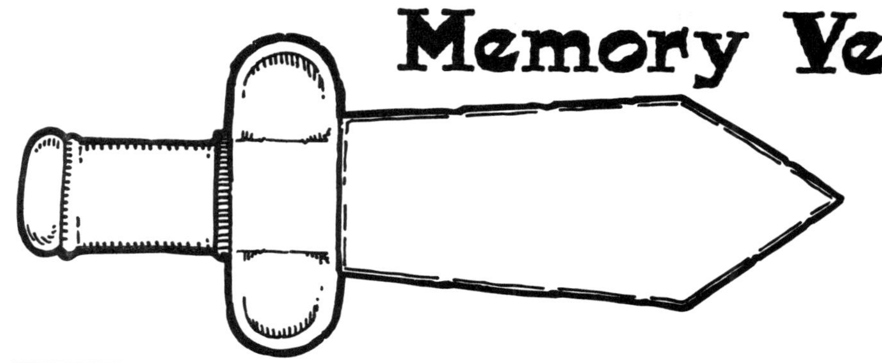

The Lord is good to all. Psalm 145:9a	*Give thanks . . .* 1 Thessalonians 5:18a	*Help me, O Lord my God.* Psalm 109:26a	*. . . "The Lord is my helper; I will not be afraid."* Hebrews 13:6a
. . . Believe that Jesus is the Christ, the Son of God. John 20:31a	*As for God, his way is perfect.* Psalm 18:30a	*". . . Repent and be baptized, every one of you, in the name of Jesus Christ."* Acts 2:38a	*"It is more blessed to give than receive."* Acts 20:35b
"Watch and pray." Mark 14:38a *". . . Love one another."* John 13:34b	*Do not be overcome by evil, but overcome evil with good.* Romans 12:21	*Search me, O God, and know my heart.* Psalm 139:23a	*The gift of God is eternal life in Christ Jesus our Lord.* Romans 6:23b
The fear of the Lord is the beginning of wisdom. Psalm 111:10a	*"For the eyes of the Lord are on the righteous."* 1 Peter 3:12a	*Trust in the Lord and do good.* Psalm 37:3a	*The Lord is righteous in all his ways.* Psalm 145:17a

Soldier Puppet

Use this soldier puppet to tell others to be good Christians and wear God's armor every day.

1. Color the head. Cut it out in two pieces.
2. Glue the top of the face to the bottom of a small lunch bag as shown.
3. Glue the chin and neck to the side of the bag that is under the face as shown.
4. Put your hand in the bag, moving the bottom flap up and down to make the puppet talk.

Cut here.

Symbolic Shield

Knights and royalty used to put symbols and designs on their shields. These represented characteristics of a person or family. For example, a stag represented purity or strength; a falcon stood for bravery; and an open hand meant generosity. Even the lines and bars on the shields had special meanings.

Look at the symbols below. Design your own shield using the pattern on page 22. Use one or more of the symbols below or make up your own. It doesn't matter where you put the symbols, but try to have a balanced-looking shield.

VALOR

BEAUTY

COURAGE

SINCERITY, LOVE, AND LOYALTY

BRAVERY

CHRISTIAN

WISDOM

EAGER, OR STRENGTH OF MIND

WARRIOR

STRENGTH AND PROTECTION

HONOR

ACHIEVEMENT

Shield Pattern

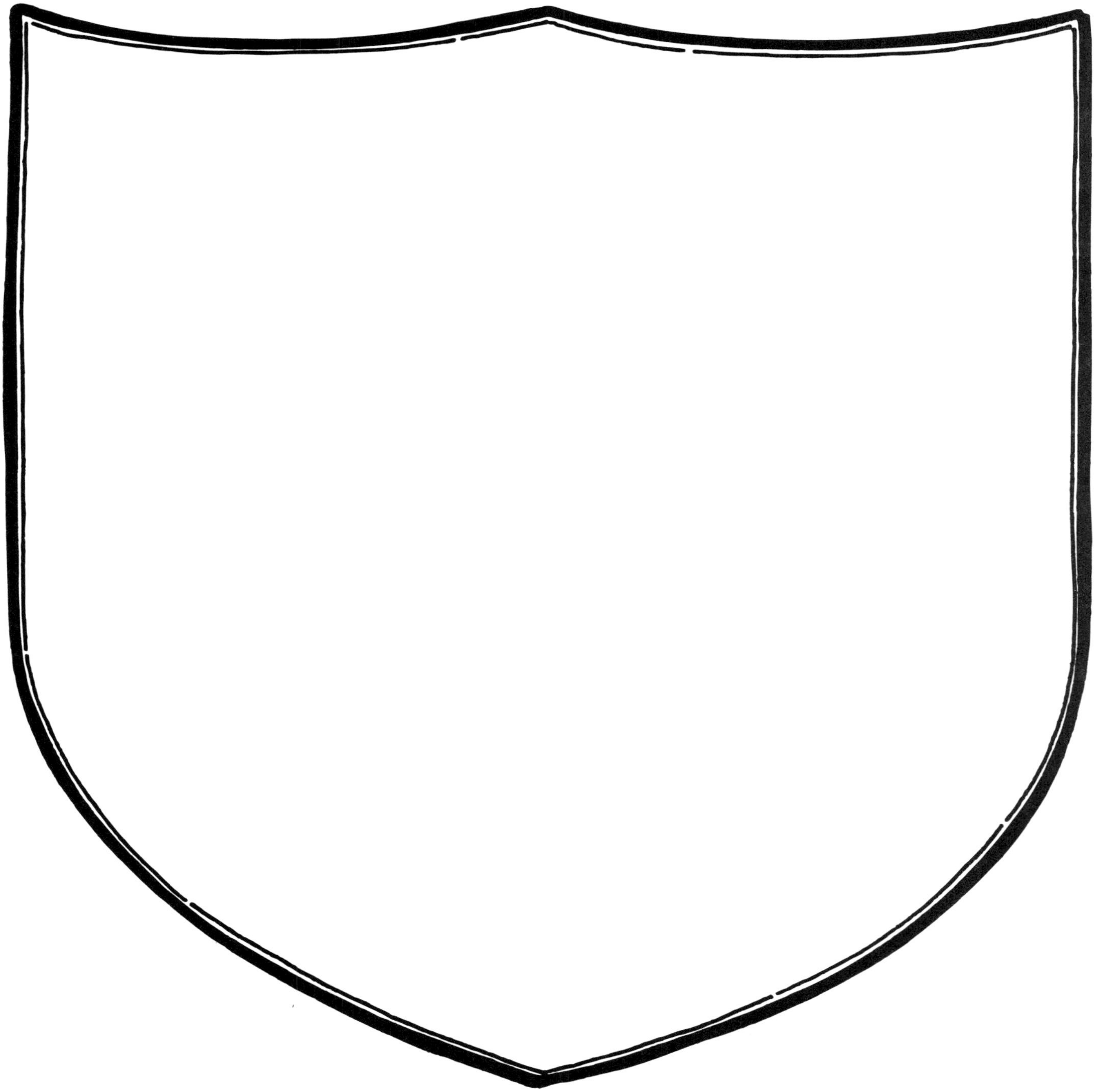

Jesus Pennant

This pennant will never let you forget who is the one true king.

1. Color and cut out the pennant.
2. Glue on the end.
3. Hang the pennant on a wall in your room.

JESUS IS MY KING

JESUS IS MY KING

"Life's Travels" Game

God gives us special armor to help us fight problems in our everyday lives. But we need to use the armor. This game will help you see when you need to use God's armor.

START

1

2 Everything's going well. Take another turn.

3 You gave in to temptation to steal. Take a detour left 1 space.

DETOUR

You returned a stolen item. Go back to space 3.

END OF DETOUR

4 You gave your life to Jesus. Take another turn.

5 Be thankful for getting this far. Go ahead 2 spaces.

6

7 You ask God to help you be a faithful soldier. Go ahead 1 space.

8

9 You got sidetracked wanting too many things. Go back 1 space.

10 You complained about going to church. Go back 1 space.

11 Your friends wanted you to steal, but you said no. Take another turn.

12

13

WELCOME

$

1. Use buttons for markers.
2. Flip a penny to move (heads = 2 spaces, tails = 1 space).
2. Try to reach heaven, the place every Christian soldier is headed for.

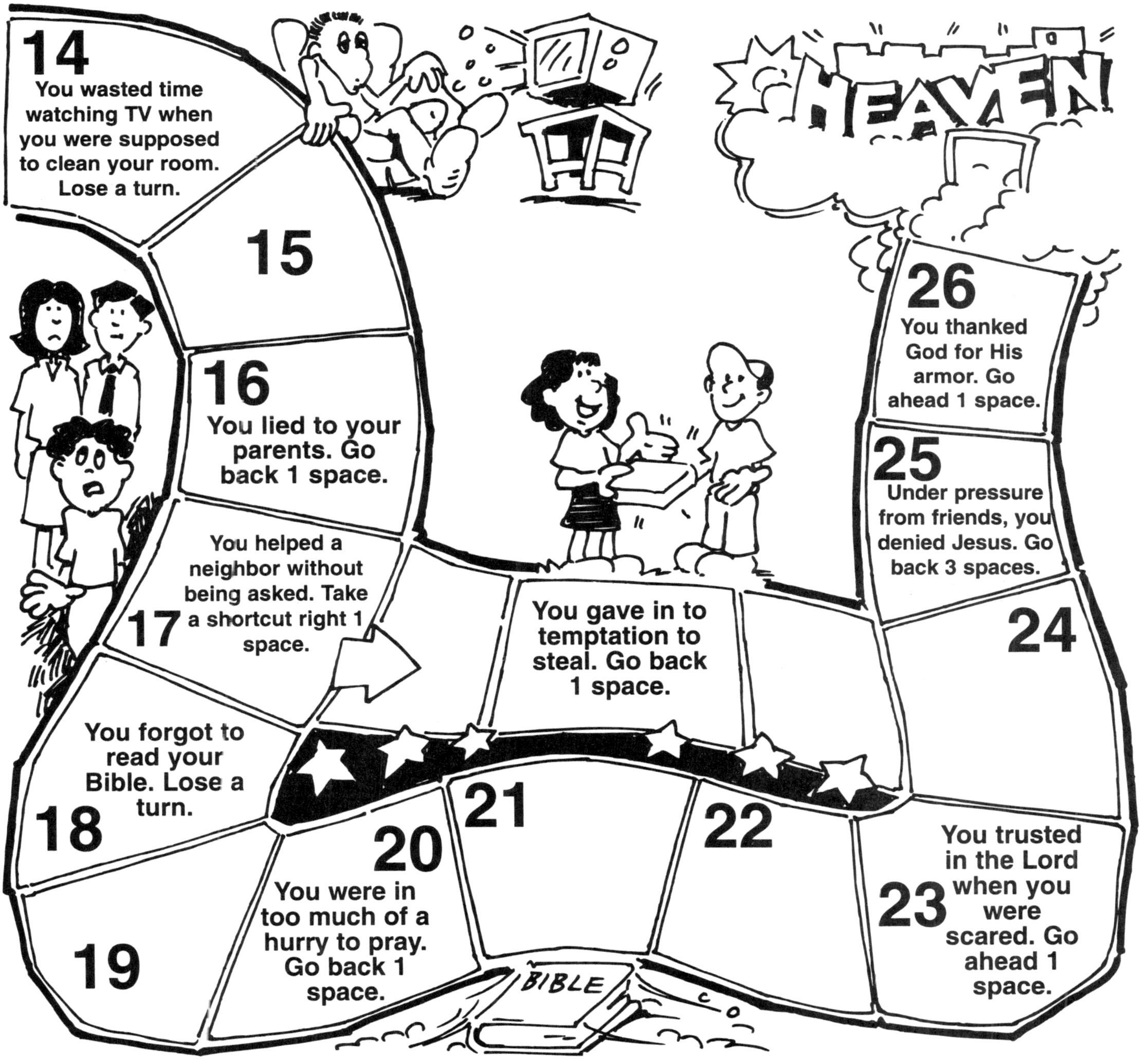

14 You wasted time watching TV when you were supposed to clean your room. Lose a turn.

15

16 You lied to your parents. Go back 1 space.

17 You helped a neighbor without being asked. Take a shortcut right 1 space.

18 You forgot to read your Bible. Lose a turn.

19

20 You were in too much of a hurry to pray. Go back 1 space.

21

You gave in to temptation to steal. Go back 1 space.

22

23 You trusted in the Lord when you were scared. Go ahead 1 space.

24

25 Under pressure from friends, you denied Jesus. Go back 3 spaces.

26 You thanked God for His armor. Go ahead 1 space.

HEAVEN

BIBLE

Movable Soldier

Create your own soldier of God who wears God's armor to keep him strong against all evil.

1. Color and cut out the pieces of the soldier and the shield below and on pages 27 and 28. (You may want to glue the pieces on cardboard first to make them sturdier.)
2. Cover each piece with clear plastic adhesive, front and back.
3. Poke a hole in each piece where the black dot is.
4. Use brass fasteners to connect the pieces together.

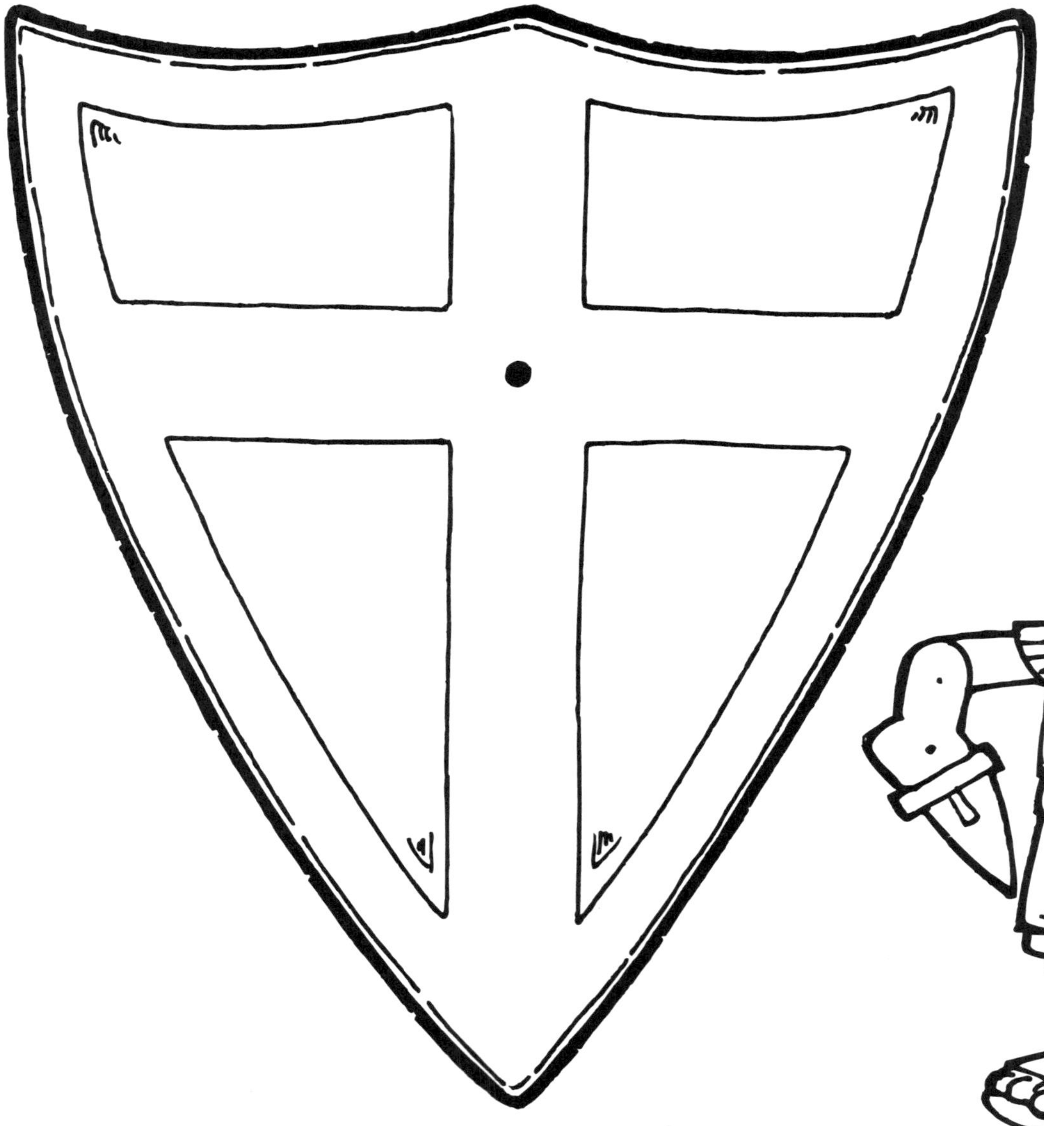

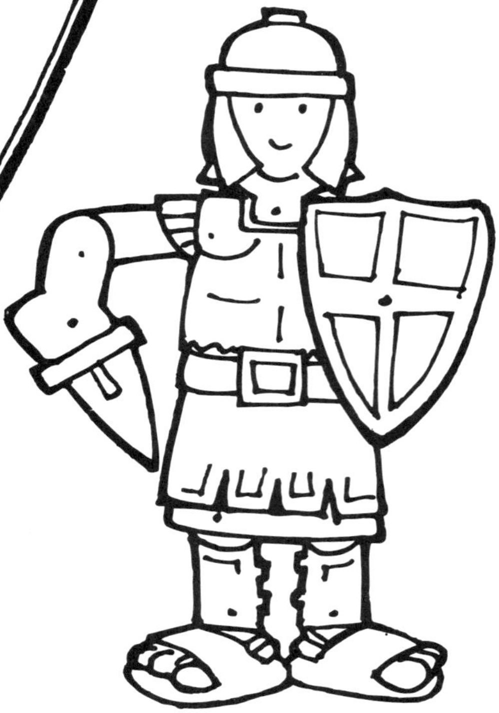

Soldier Patterns

Soldier Patterns

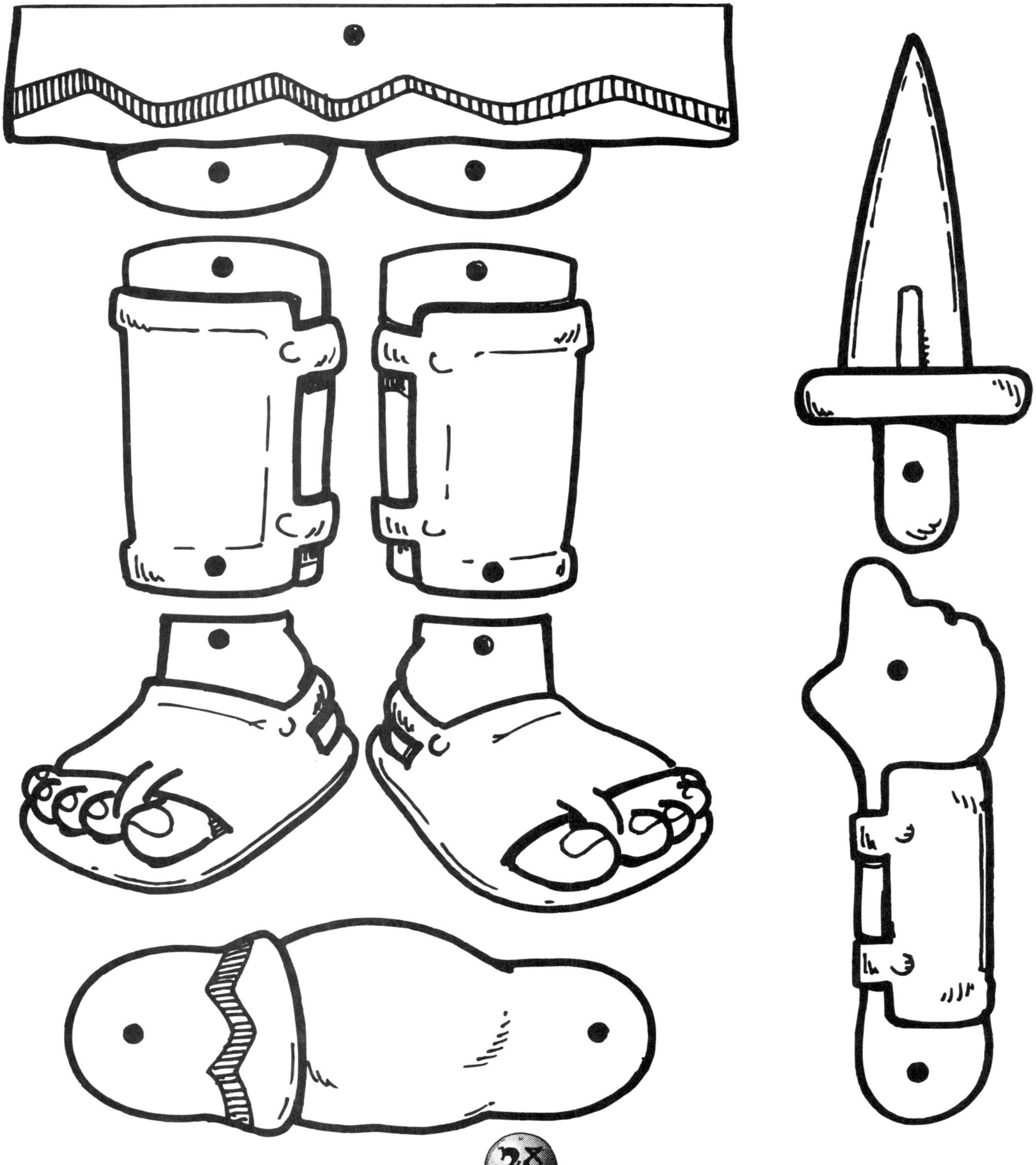

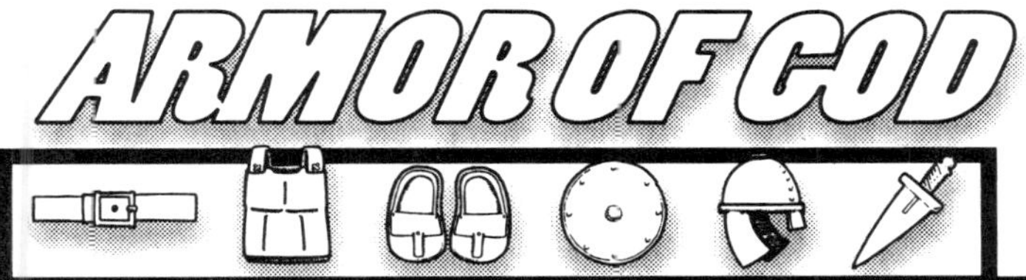

A Christian's Pledge

Set this pledge up in your room to remind you of your duties as a soldier of Christ.

1. Color and cut out the pledge card on the heavy lines.
2. Fold on the dotted line.

LOVE GOD—HATE EVIL

Forgetting
All,
I
Trust
Him.

Fold.

CHRISTIAN'S PLEDGE

I, ______________________, promise not to follow
(Your name here.)

the world, but to be true to Jesus Christ who gave His life for me.

I will do my best to obey His Word and love God and others. I trust God with my life and want to serve Him. I will not be afraid to stand up for the Lord.

Crown of Righteousness

God promised that everyone who believes in Jesus will one day receive a crown of righteousness (2 Timothy 4:8). Make this crown as a reminder that one day, you'll have a real one.

1. Color and cut out the crown pieces on page 31. (You may want to glue them onto cardboard first to make them sturdier.) Make two copies of the headband.
2. Tape the headbands to the front to make the crown fit your head.

Crown Patterns

Make two copies of this headband.

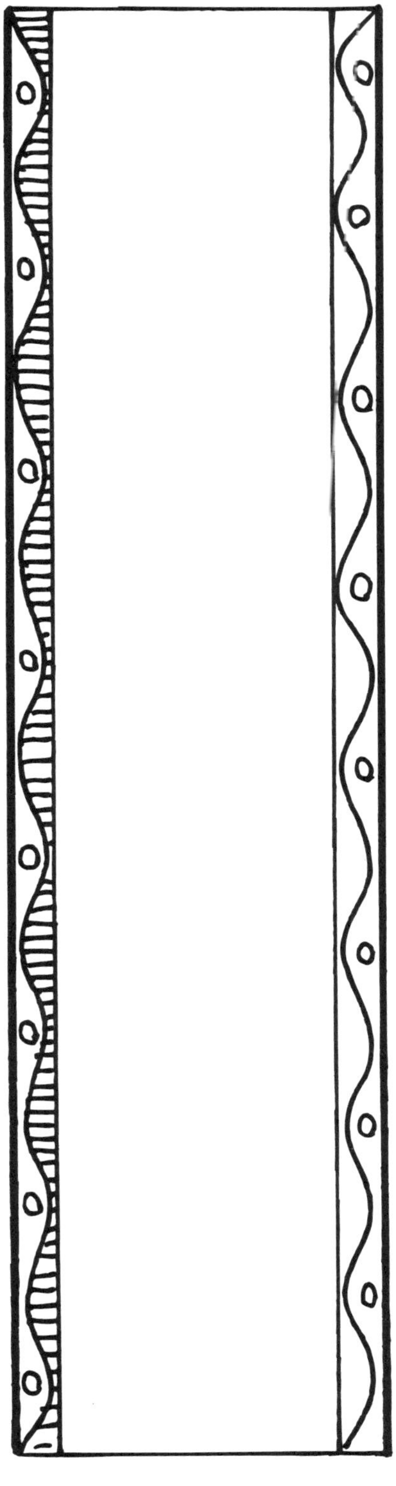

. . . "Be faithful, even to the point of death, and I will give you the crown of life." Revelation 2:10b

Foil Shield

Make this shield as a reminder of the help God gives us against temptation.

1. Draw a shield shape on heavy cardboard.
2. Glue a cardboard handle on the back (made from a strip of folded cardboard) as shown.
3. Draw and cut out symbols from heavy cardboard. You may trace the ones below or draw your own.
4. Glue the symbols to the shield. (You may want to add other designs such as thick heavy cord or small beads.)
5. After the glue has dried, cover the entire front of the shield with aluminum foil. Press it down firmly all over to make sure the designs stand out against the shield. It's okay if the foil is crinkled.
6. Fold the foil over the edges of the shield and glue it in place on the back.

Citizenship Certificate

If you have received Jesus as your Savior, you are a citizen of heaven!

1. Glue or draw a small picture of yourself in the box on the certificate below. Write your name under the picture.
2. Cut out the certificate.
3. Color the border.
4. Roll up the certificate and tie it with a 9" piece of red ribbon.

Certificate of Citizenship in the Kingdom of Heaven

This certifies that

____

has completed the requirements in the Word of God to be a child of God and is awarded a home in heaven.

HOLY SPIRIT

Jesus Christ

GOD'S SON

Stand-up Castle

We can find great strength in God, for He is a mighty fortress, like a castle.

1. Color the castle pieces and soldiers below and on page 35.
2. Glue them to lightweight cardboard.
3. Cut out all the pieces.
4. Fold the castle pieces on the dotted lines and glue them together.
5. Fold the tab on each soldier to make him stand up.

TAB

TAB

Place glued tab behind B.

C

Apply glue here.

A MIGHTY FORTRESS IS OUR GOD

Castle Patterns

TAB

TAB

TAB

TAB

TAB

Place glued tab behind C.

Apply glue here.

Apply glue here.

B

Armor Shaped Cookies

These cookies are a delicious and fun way to think about God's armor.

Ingredients:

½ cup butter
1 cup sugar
1 egg
½ tsp. vanilla
2 ½ cups flour
½ tsp. salt
1 ½ tsp. baking soda
2 tbs. milk

1. Cream butter and sugar.
2. Add egg and vanilla and beat well.
3. Add flour, salt, baking soda, and milk.
4. When thoroughly mixed, chill dough for 2 hours.
5. Roll chilled dough ⅓" thick on lightly floured board.
6. Cut out the armor patterns on page 37.
7. Lay the patterns on the cookie dough. Carefully cut around each one with a knife.
8. Carefully lift cookies from board and place them on an ungreased cookie sheet.
9. Bake cookies at 400 degrees for 8–10 minutes.
10. Let cookies cool on a wire rack or sheet of waxed paper.
11. Frost with vanilla frosting. (To make your own frosting, mix powered sugar, milk, and a little butter until it's the right consistency.)
12. Decorate cookies with sprinkles and silver balls.

SS4875

Armor Cookie Patterns

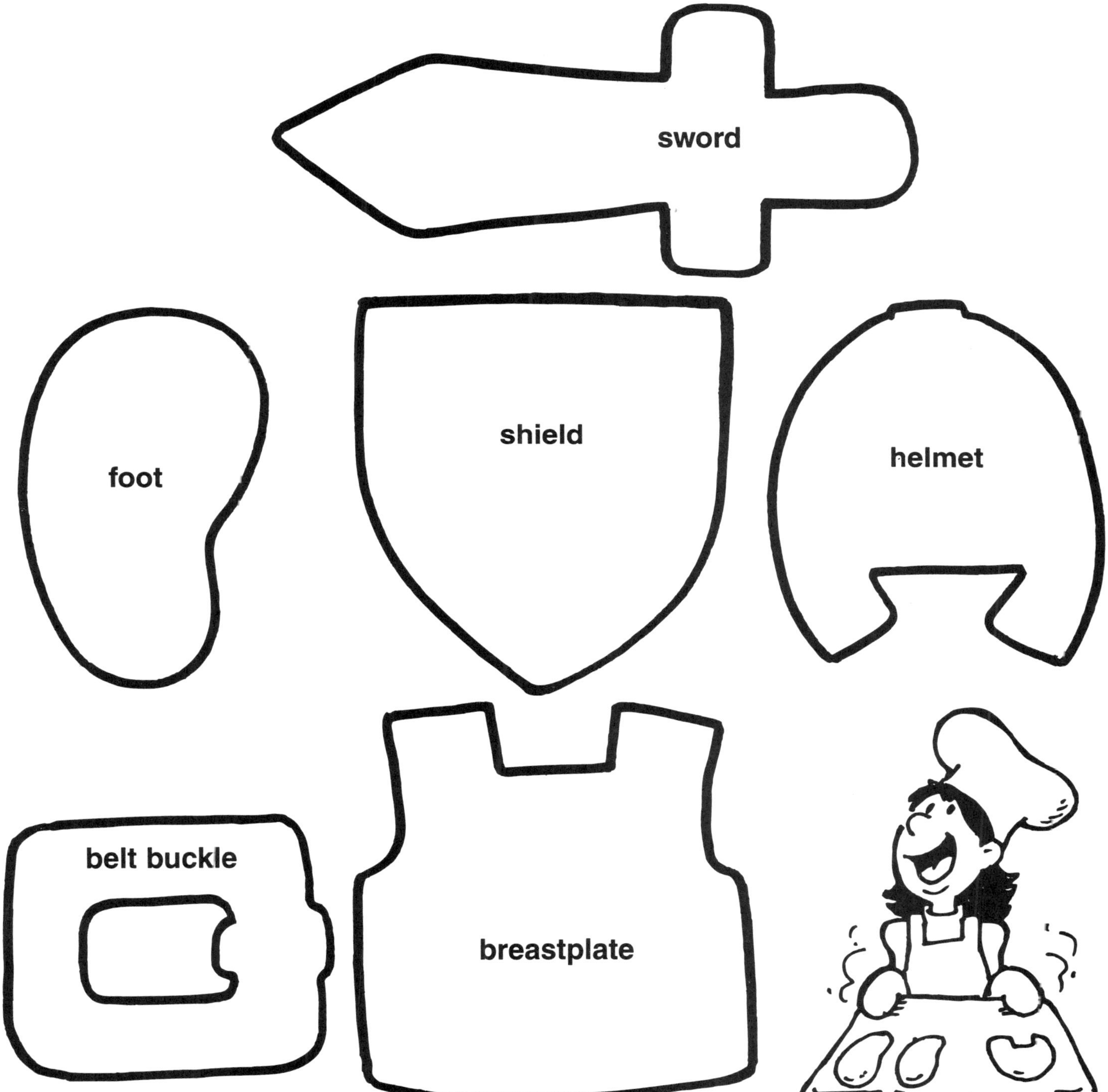

sword

foot

shield

helmet

belt buckle

breastplate

"Look to Jesus" Bulletin Board

1. Color and cut out the patterns below and on pages 39–41.
2. Trace the letters on black construction paper to spell out the bulletin board title, "Look to Jesus."
3. Cut out the letters.
4. Mount the letters and patterns on a bulletin board or a large piece of posterboard as shown.

L u K

O E S

Bulletin Board Patterns

Bulletin Board Patterns

J

Bulletin Board Pattern

Let us fix our eyes on

JESUS,

the

AUTHOR

and

PERFECTER

of our

FAITH . . .

Hebrews 12:2a

A Soldier's Song

Many of the hymns and choruses we sing in church are about being soldiers of Christ. Read the words of the hymn below. Sing the hymn with your friends and family.

George Duffield, Jr.

George J. Webb

1. Stand up, stand up for Je - sus, Ye sol - diers of the cross;
2. Stand up, stand up for Je - sus, Stand in his strength a - lone;

Lift high his roy - al ban - ner, It must not suf - fer loss;
The arm of flesh will fail you, Ye dare not trust your own;

From vic - tory un - to vic - tory His ar - my shall he lead,
Put on the gos - pel ar - mor, Each piece put on with prayer;

Till ev - ery foe is van - quished, And Christ is Lord in - deed.
Where du - ty calls or dan - ger, Be nev - er want - ing there.

A Poster to Color

Color and hang this poster in your room to remind you to follow God's laws.

CHOOSE LIFE

ETERNAL LIFE

ETERNAL DEATH

Which road are you taking?

Jesus Christ is the only way to heaven.

Armor of God Plaque

paper strips

This plaque will add a nice touch to your room where it can remind you to "put on" each piece of God's armor first thing every morning.

1. Color and cut out the pieces of armor on page 45.
2. Trace around the paper strips on black or gold construction paper and cut them out.
3. Glue the strips together to make one long strip.
4. Cut out the word card below.
5. Glue the word card and pieces of armor on the strip as shown.

Put on the Whole Armor of God.

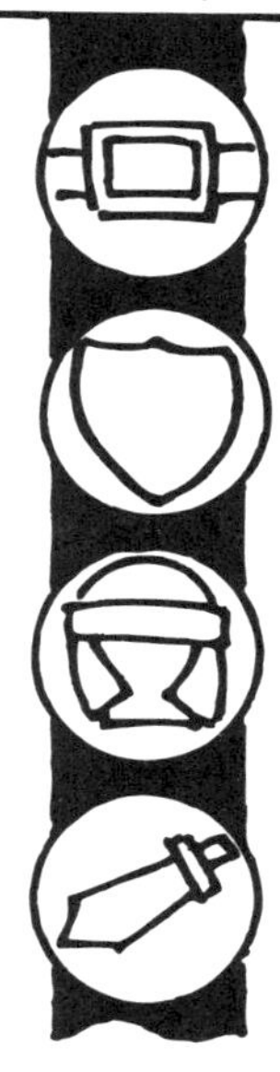

Put on the Whole Armor of God

Plaque Pieces

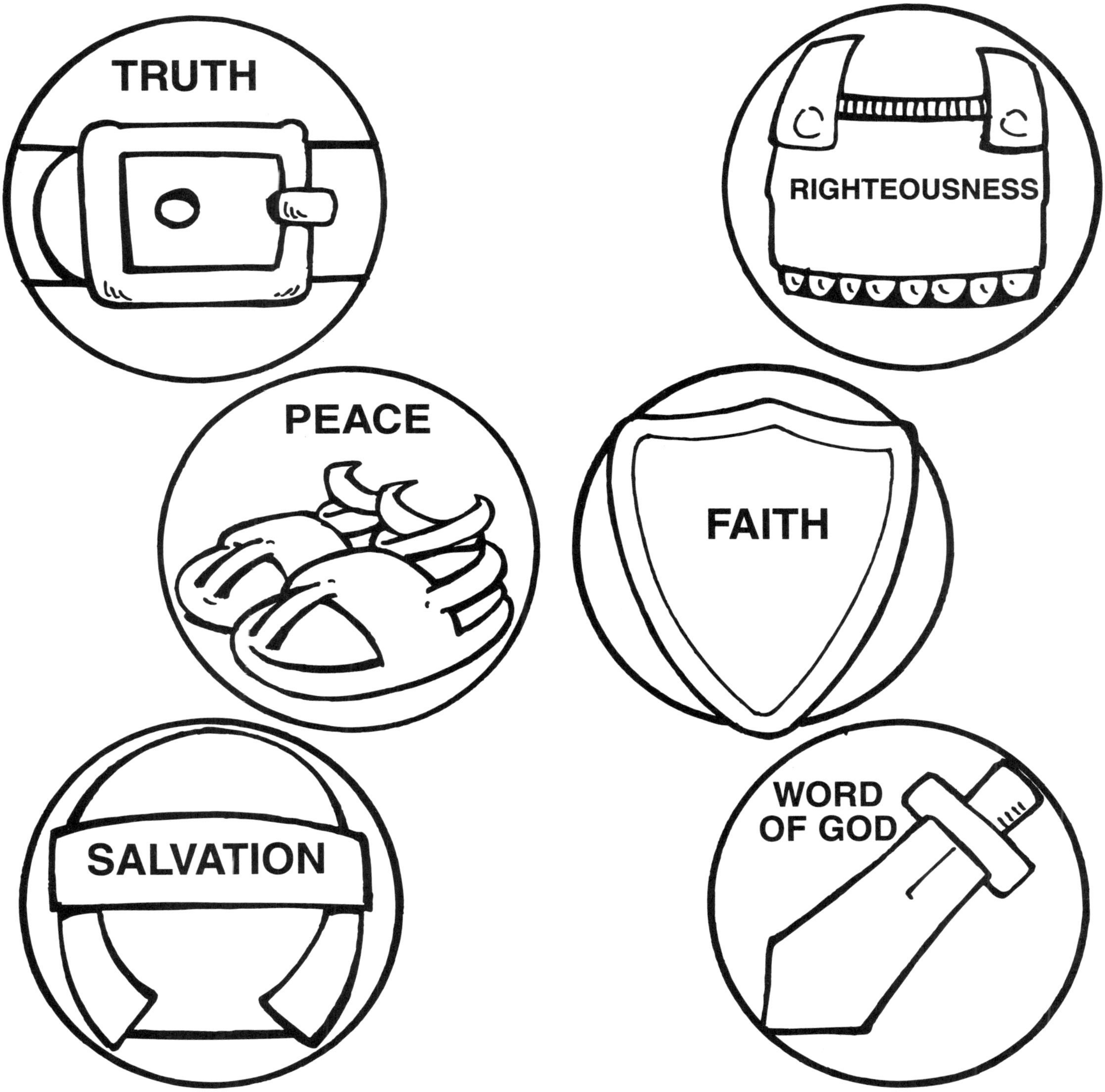

TRUTH

RIGHTEOUSNESS

PEACE

FAITH

SALVATION

WORD OF GOD

Christian Soldier Mini-Book

1. Color the pictures below and on pages 47–48.
2. Cut out the pictures.
3. Fold three 8½" x 11" pieces of paper in half.
4. Put the folded sheets together to make a mini-book. Number the pages 1–12 (the front of the book will be page 1 and the back will be page 12.)
5. Decorate the front page and print on it "What does a Christian soldier do?"
6. Open the book to pages 2 and 3.
7. On page 2, print the following: "A Christian soldier . . ."
8. Glue one of the pictures to page 3.
9. Continue this way throughout the book, writing "A Christian soldier . . ." on every even page and gluing a picture to every odd page.
10. Staple the pages together to complete your mini-book.
11. Decorate the last page any way you choose.

Mini-Book Pictures

Mini-Book Pictures

sings hymns and spiritual songs

obeys happily